This book ~~belongs to:~~ *is shared with*

____

____

____

the hug who got stuck

to all who hug

Illustrations by Alexis Aronson

Published by
Conscious Stories LLC
4800 Baseline Rd,
Suite E104-365
Boulder, CO
80303
USA

www.consciousstories.com

First Edition
Library of Congress
Control Number: 2017901959
ISBN 978-1-943750-20-7

The last 20 minutes of every day are precious.

Dear parents, teachers, and readers,

This story has been gift-wrapped with two simple mindfulness practices to help you connect more deeply with your children in the last 20 minutes of each day.

- Quietly set your intention for calm and open connection.
- Then start your story time with the **Snuggle Breathing Meditation**. Read each line aloud and take slow deep breaths together. This can be very relaxing and help everyone settle.
- At the end of the story, you will find your **Daily Hug Meter**. If your children (or you) are low on hugs for the day, now is the time to catch up before sleep. It is also an opportunity to remember the people whom you loved today and those you are going to give love to tomorrow. Please don't skip this. It helps to create belonging and heal feelings of loneliness.

Enjoy snuggling into togetherness!

Andrew

An easy breathing meditation

Snuggle Breathing

Our story begins with us breathing together.
Say each line aloud and then
take a slow deep breath in and out.

I breathe for me

I breathe for you

I breathe for us

I breathe for all that surrounds us

Once upon a time,
on a very ordinary day,
deep in the center
of a very ordinary heart …

an...

extraordinary...

thing...

happened.

Reminders to being a Great Hug

Deep in the center
of this heart
was a Hug Factory.

The Hug Factory
made the most warm,
cozy, cuddly hugs.

Reminders to being a Great Hug
1 Breathe in love to glow brightly.
2 Focus entirely on the heart the love is for.
3 Don't pay too much attention to The Web of Sticky Thoughts.
11

Each hug was freshly made
and specially encoded
with just the right amount
of love and care
to delight the heart
it was made for.

Being a hug wasn't always easy.

Sometimes a lonely thought
or bad feeling would trap
a hug in a sticky web.

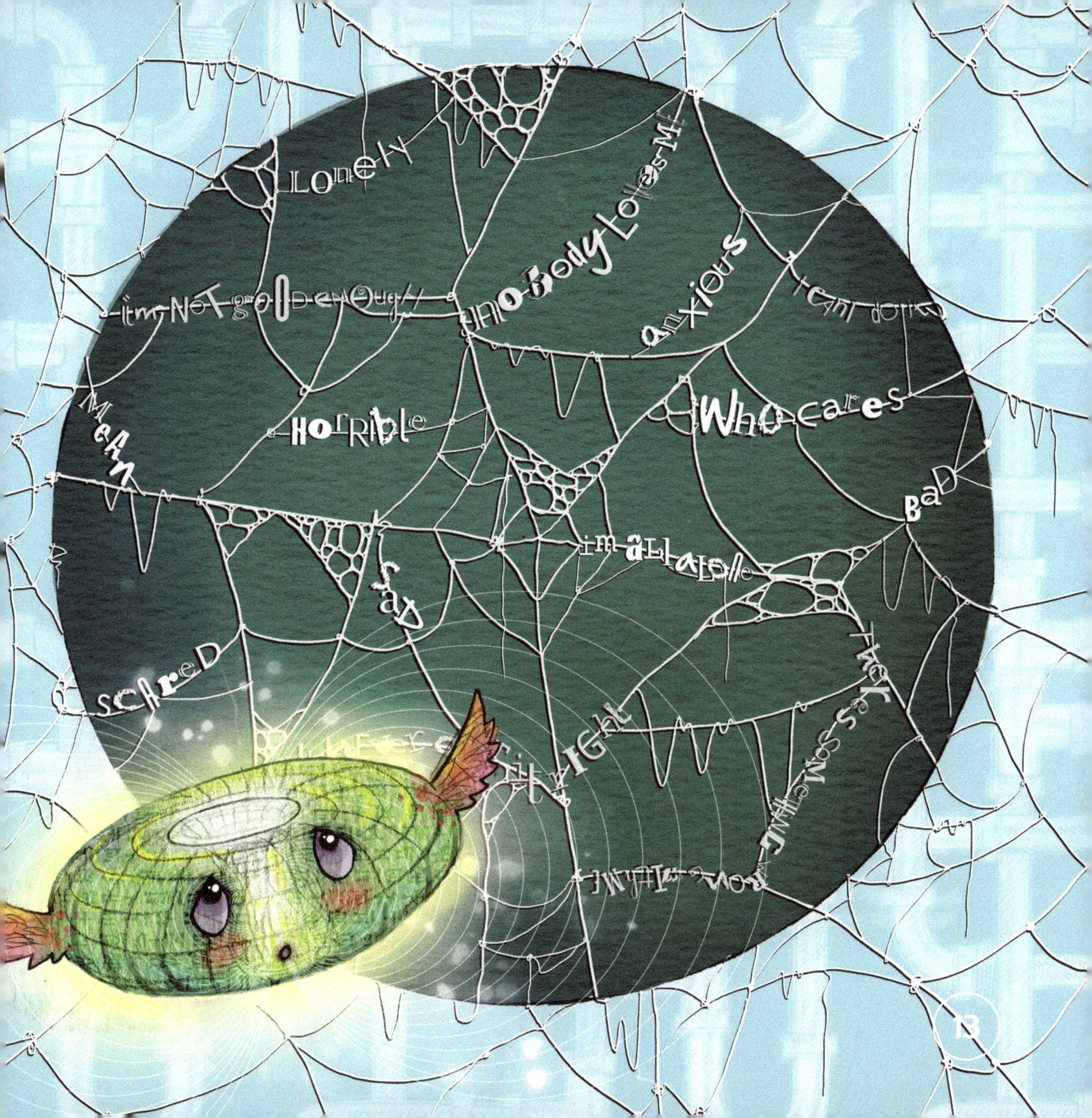
Lonely
Nobody Loves Me
anxious
I can't do it
I'm Not good enough
Mean
Horrible
Who cares
Bad
Sad
scared
There's something wrong with me

So, to help hugs deliver their love and care, there was a big sign on the factory wall:

Reminders to being a Great Hug

1. Breathe in love to glow brightly.

2. Focus entirely on the heart the love is for.

3. Don't pay too much attention to The Web of Sticky Thoughts.

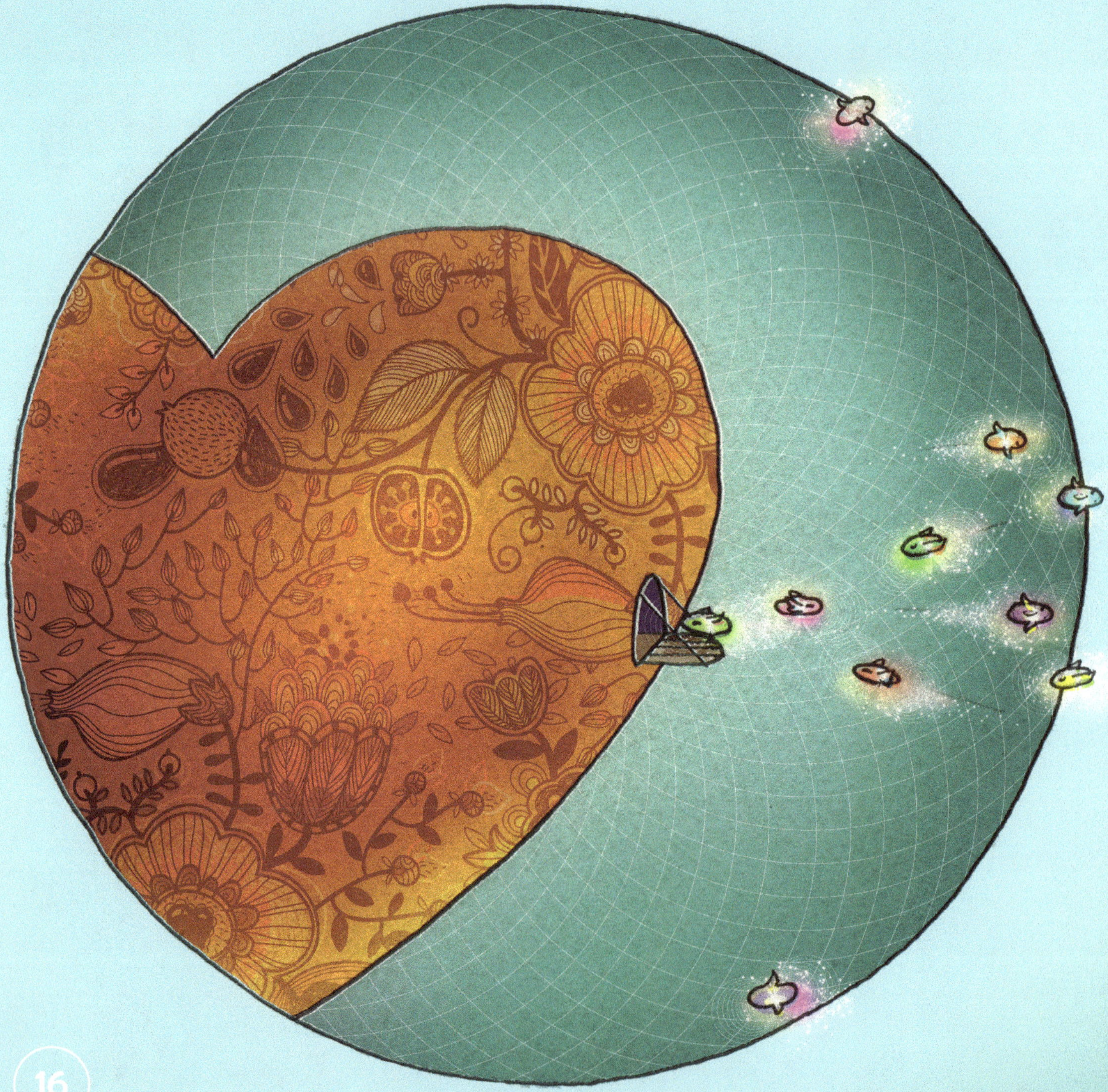

On most days you could see streams of hugs entering and leaving the door of the heart, zooming away like bees from a hive, but not on this day.

On this day there was a problem ...

One special hug, on its way
out of the heart, got stuck.

Very, very stuck.

I can't do it
Sad
Mean
Horrible
anxious
Who cares
Bad
scared
Lonely
Not good enough

This hug had forgotten
the third rule!

It fought against The Web of
Sticky Thoughts to get free,
but every wriggle and squirm
trapped the hug even more.

Soon the hug
ran out of breath
and lost its glow.

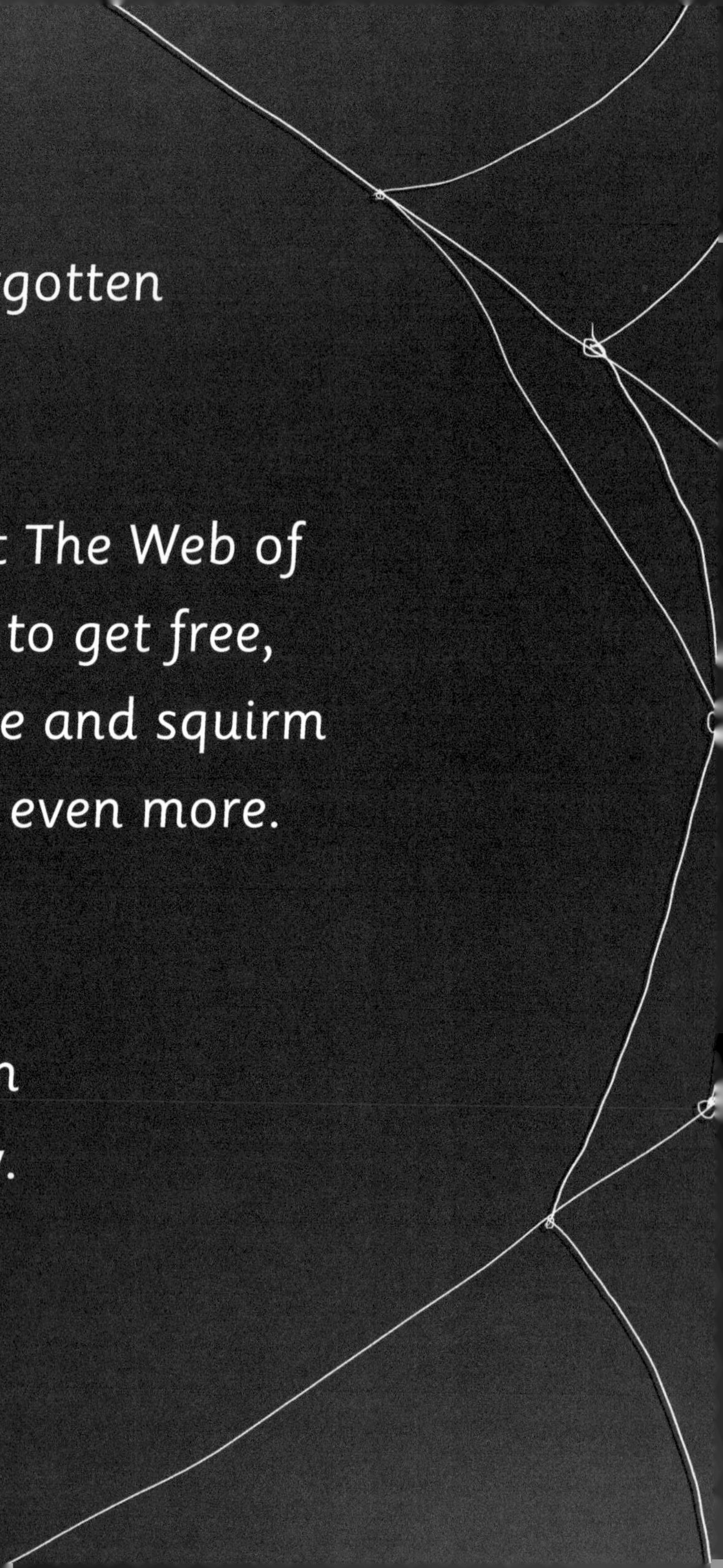

mean
inadequate
Get it right
Lonely
Nobody Loves Me
There's something wrong with me
Who cares
bad
I can't do it
I'm not good enough
anxious

Inside, the heart became horribly congested with crowds of hugs waiting to get out.

Unused hugs were put into boxes until every inch of space was filled up.

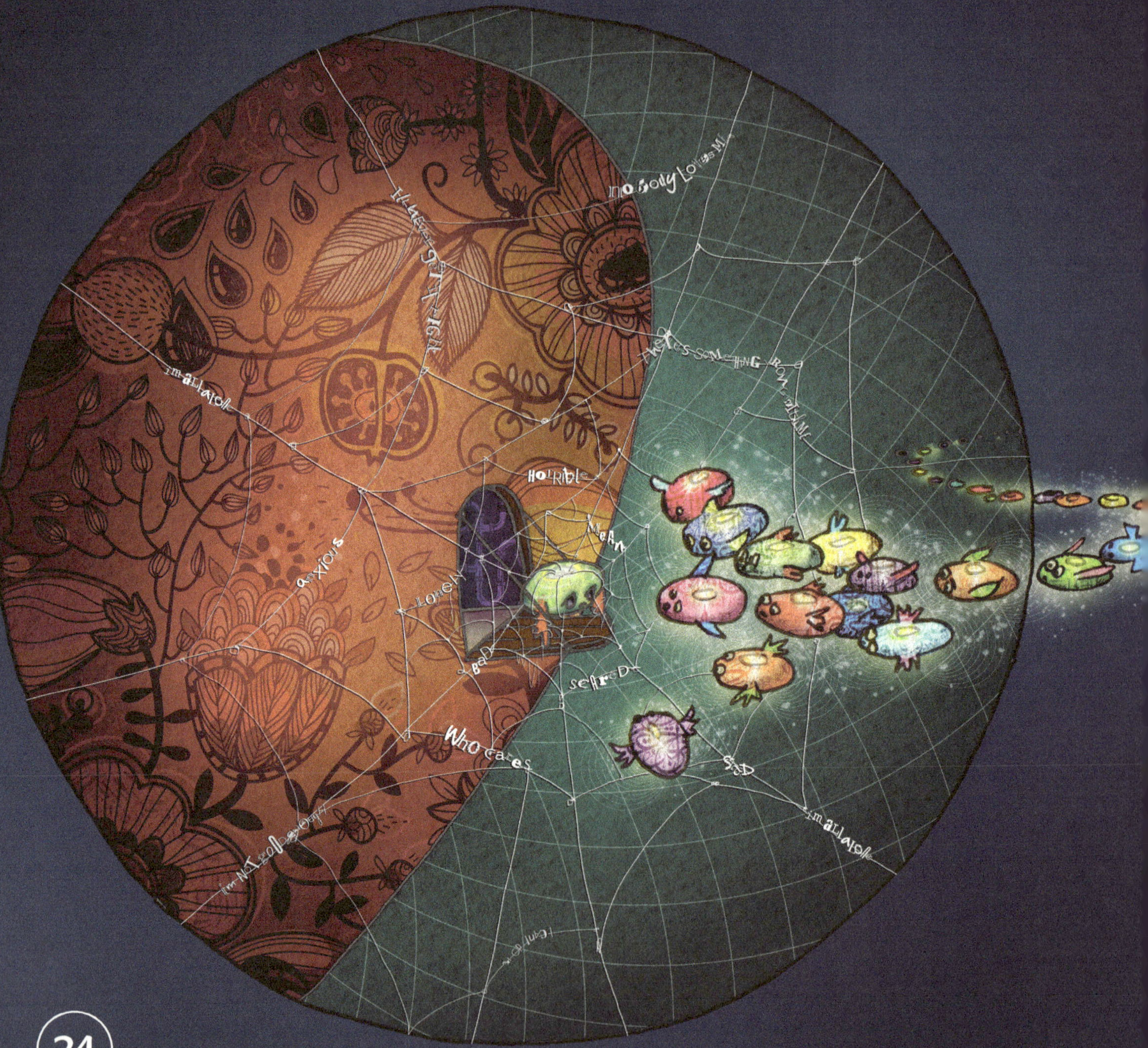
nobody loves me
Horrible
Mean
anxious
Bad
Scared
Who cares
Sad

Outside the heart there was also a problem.

A traffic jam of visiting hugs couldn't get in to deliver their special love and care.

Soon the factory stopped making new hugs.

There was only one stuck hug
in the center of one ordinary
heart, but all around the world,
hugs lost a little of their glow.

The hug sighed helplessly.

It stopped wriggling,
stopped squirming,
and stopped fighting.

In that moment something magical happened.

Who cares
Lonely

As it stopped wriggling...
it breathed in love
and glowed brighter.

As it stopped squirming...
it remembered the heart
it was made for.

As it stopped fighting...
it slipped right past The Web
of Sticky Thoughts.

FREE!

The hug glowed
brighter and brighter...

zooming away toward
the one special heart
it was made for.

Reminders to being a Great Hug
1 Breathe in love to glow brightly.
2 Focus entirely on the heart the love is for.
3 Don't pay too much attention to The Web of Sticky Thoughts.

The Hug Factory clinked
and whirled back to life.
A flood of hugs passed in and
out of the heart, each delivering
their special love and care.

It was just one hug
who got unstuck
in the center
of one ordinary heart,
and all around the world,
an extraordinary
softening happened.

> **"We need four hugs a day for survival. We need eight hugs a day for maintenance. We need twelve hugs a day for growth."**
>
> **– Virginia Satir**
> **The 'Mother of Family Therapy'**

Does your heart feel full or would you like another hug?

Have fun answering these questions together as you end your day with a full and happy heart.

Filling up on hugs

Your Daily Hug Meter

2 **How many hugs did you give today?**

1 **How many hugs did you receive today?**

3 What special ingredients do you put into your hugs?

4 What sticky thoughts are bothering you?

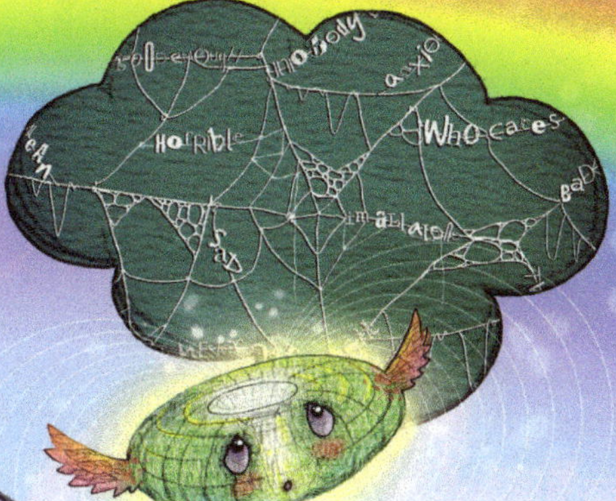

5 Do you remember how to get free? Let's do that together now.

6 Who are you growing hugs for as you sleep snuggly tonight?

Free downloadable coloring pages and monthly full-moon storytime

Visit www.consciousstories.com for details

#consciousbedtimestories

@Conscious Bedtime Story Club

Andrew Newman - author

Andrew Newman is the award-winning author and founder of www.ConsciousStories.com, a growing series of bedtime stories purpose-built to support parent-child connection in the last 20 minutes of the day. His professional background includes deep training in therapeutic healing work and mindfulness. He brings a calm yet playful energy to speaking events and workshops, inviting and encouraging the creativity of his audiences, children K-5, parents, and teachers alike.

Andrew has been an opening speaker for Deepak Chopra, a TEDx presenter in Findhorn, Scotland and author-in-residence at the Bixby School in Boulder, Colorado. He is a graduate of The Barbara Brennan School of Healing, a Non-Dual Kabbalistic healer and has been actively involved in men's work through the Mankind Project since 2006. He counsels parents, helping them to return to their center, so they can be more deeply present with their kids.

TEDx **"Why the last 20 minutes of the day matter"**

Alexis Aronson – illustrator

Alexis is a self-taught illustrator, designer and artist from Cape Town, South Africa. She has a passion for serving projects with a visionary twist that incorporate image making with the growth of human consciousness for broader impact. Her media range from digital illustration and design to fine art techniques, such as intaglio printmaking, ceramic sculpture, and painting. In between working for clients and creating her own art for exhibition, Alexis is an avid nature lover, swimmer, yogi, hiker, and gardener.

www.alexisaronson.com

Star Counter

Every time you breathe together and read aloud, you make a star shine in the night sky.

Color in a star to count how many times you have read this book.

CPSIA information can be obtained
at www.ICGtesting.com
Printed in the USA
LVHW071134071122
732538LV00009B/103

9 781943 750207